Written by Mary McKelvey

Illustrated by Daniel Rodgers

Lake District Press

Lake District Press
First published in Great Britain in 2008 by Lake District Press
Cumbria

Book design and illustrations © ICAN DESIGN LTD, 2008
www.icandesign.co.uk
Text © Lake District Press, 2008
The text for this book is set in Carmina.
The colour paintings are rendered in oil paint.
The pen and ink artwork is coloured digitally.

A CIP catalogue record for this book is available from the British Library.

ISBN: 978-0-9556493-0-1

Printed in China

SPELLING MAGIC

This book belongs to:

....

CONTENTS – spelling activities for **highlighted** words

Dear parent,

The material in Spelling Magic is designed to give children confidence in spelling 'problem' words. These words include ones that have an unusual letter pattern, silent letters, or different letters to those indicated by the sound.

The strategies in Spelling Magic involve close observation of words, linking unknown spellings to known spellings, and the use of memory rhymes to spell out words letter by letter.

Appearing throughout this book is Bertie the Spelling Magician, a humorous rabbit character, whose antics will appeal to its young audience. Spotting what Bertie is up to on each page draws attention to the illustrations, which are an essential aid to the remembering process for each of the words whose accurate spelling needs to be learned.

Spelling Magic offers challenging, interesting material, which promotes spelling success with words that cause many children problems.

How to use this book

 Work through the material with your child giving support and encouragement.

 The content of the book is not designed to be rushed through. Remind your child of the tortoise and the hare story; the tortoise's steady plodding won the day over the hare's rushing.

 There is no set order in which to learn the spelling of these words. Let your child choose which are the best words to master first.

 Ensure your child has grasped the correct spelling of one word before moving on to another word.

 As each new spelling is learned, revisit ones already covered and check your child still has the accurate spelling of these words at hand.

 Making and displaying a poster can help your child master the spelling of a word.

 Praise the achievement of the grasp of each new word and see your child grow in spelling confidence.

Hello

Hello. I'm Bertie the Spelling Magician, and there is no spelling problem that I cannot help you solve. In this book I am going to show you tricks and tips that will help you spell correctly every time.

I will teach you how to spell a variety of words that are difficult because some of the letters in these words are not what you would expect. To help you learn how to spell these words correctly I will:

* Show you how words are made up

* Show you how to spell one word which then lets you spell other words using the same letter pattern

* Give you spelling rhymes to help you remember the order of letters in words

children!

I will tell you why certain words are hard to spell and how they are commonly misspelled. I have also set some fun activities for you to do to make sure you will learn the exact spelling of each word.

The pictures are really important too. Think of the picture for each word; it helps to remind you what you have to remember.

Look out for me in each of the pictures and see what I am getting up to on each page. Sometimes I'm an action rabbit, sometimes I'm a bit naughty, but I'm never boring and always memorable.

Now turn over the pages and begin your training to become a Spelling Magician like me.

said

It is difficult to spell **said** correctly. It sounds like it should be spelled **sed**. The **ai** in **said** gives you the **e** sound you hear.

You could remember the letters in **said** by knowing that **said** is **sad** with **i** slotted in between the **sa** and the **d**.

sad becomes **said**

ACTIVITY

Draw your own picture of Alan. Show him in a dangerous situation.

In a speech bubble coming from him, put the words, '**it's dangerous**'.

Write on your picture how you can remember the correct spelling of **said**.

walk & talk

You can misspell **walk** and **talk** such as **worc** and **torc** because of the sounds you hear within these words.

The **alk** letter pattern in **walk** and **talk** is quite hard to grasp, but the spelling rhymes below will help you to put **alk** after **w**, and after **t**, to spell **walk** and **talk** correctly.

The **walk** spelling rhyme is **walk around little king**

The **talk** spelling rhyme is **talk about little king**

Pay particular attention to **around** in the **walk** rhyme and **about** in the **talk** rhyme. Be word perfect as you recite each rhyme to recall the letters in **walk** and **talk**.

w alk
a round
l ittle
k ing

t alk
a bout
l ittle
k ing

ACTIVITY

★ You can draw one picture to illustrate the **walk** and **talk** spelling rhymes. First of all, draw a little king in the centre of your page.

★ Then draw some people, who walk around the little king and talk about the little king. Arrows can be used to show the route the people walk around the little king. Speech bubbles can show what the people say as they talk about the little king.

★ Write the spelling rhymes for **walk** and **talk** on either side of your picture.

people

If you want to spell **people** successfully and avoid writing it as **pepul**, here is how you can do this.

Think of two people, Penny and Paul, who have different tastes in what they like to eat. Penny and Paul play for a mixed football team. At half-time they have refreshments.

Penny eats oranges, Paul likes eggs

The first letter of each of the words detailing what Paul and Penny eat will give you the correct spelling for **people**.

p enny
e ats
o ranges
p aul
l ikes
e ggs

Draw Penny scoring a goal after sensibly eating an orange, whilst Paul is bent over with a stitch after scoffing some eggs.

Bring to mind the eating habits of Penny and Paul at a football match to remember the order of letters that make up the word *people*.

ACTIVITY

could

Spelling **could** as **cud** is a very common mistake, as the **o** and the **l** are left out because they cannot be heard.

To avoid the mistake of spelling **could** as **cud**, try this method to help you remember how to spell **could** properly.

cold becomes **could**

Look closely and you will see that **could** is **cold** with **u** slotted in the middle. It is not difficult to spell **cold** and by remembering to slot **u** in the middle, you have the formula for writing **could**.

By being able to spell **could** accurately, you then have the tools to be able to spell **would** and **should**, as these have the same end-letter pattern. Try making the connection of **cold** to **could**, and then **could** to **would** and **should** with the ditty on the next page.

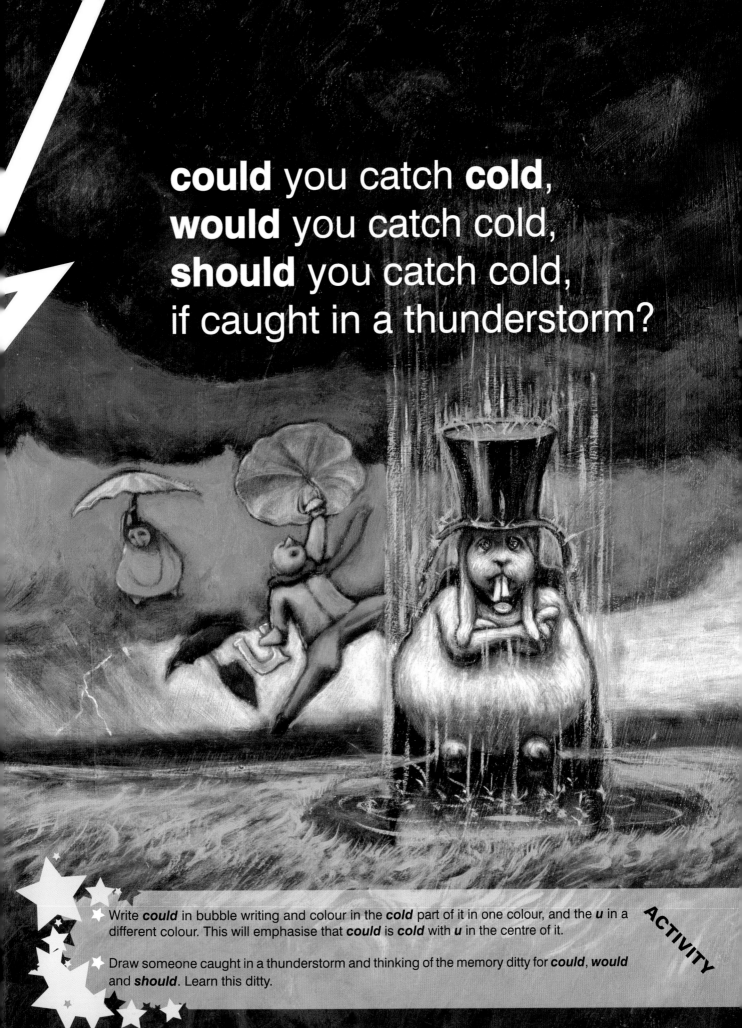

could you catch **cold**,
would you catch cold,
should you catch cold,
if caught in a thunderstorm?

ACTIVITY

Write **could** in bubble writing and colour in the **cold** part of it in one colour, and the **u** in a different colour. This will emphasise that **could** is **cold** with **u** in the centre of it.

Draw someone caught in a thunderstorm and thinking of the memory ditty for **could**, **would** and **should**. Learn this ditty.

come & some

The words **come** and **some** can be problem words, sometimes being spelt as **cum** or **cume** and **sum** or **sume**.

To remind you of the correct letter pattern for **come** and **some**, link them to the word **home**, which has the same letter pattern and is easier to spell well.

come

home

some

Think of you saying to your best friend after school, '**come home for some tea**.'

This invitation will link **come**, **home** and **some** together in your memory bank. It will help you to remember that they all belong to the **ome** family of words.

come home for some tea

ACTIVITY

Draw a picture of yourself inviting your best friend to tea.

In a speech bubble coming from you write, '**come home for some tea**.'

The invitation '**come home for some tea**' reminds you that *come* and *some* have the same *ome* letter pattern as *home*.

night

To remember that **night** has an **ight** letter pattern, rather than the **ite** letter pattern of words such as **bite** and **kite**, you can think of the spelling rhyme opposite and below.

The spelling rhyme devised for **night** is: **I will spend the**

night in grey haunted tower

This spelling rhyme reminds you of the order of letters in **night**, particularly the **ight** part of it. Whenever **gh** is followed by **t**, the **gh** is silent. If you apply this to **night**, you see that **n** says its sound, **i** says its name, **gh** is silent and **t** says its sound.

I will spend the

n ight

i n

g rey

h aunted

t ower

The **good night** message below draws your attention to three other words with the same **ight** letter pattern as **night**.

Good **night**, sleep **tight**.
What a **fright** you've had **tonight**!

ACTIVITY

Draw yourself going towards a tower with an overnight bag. To show it is night-time, draw stars and the moon and make it dark outside. Colour the tower grey and, to make it haunted, give it a ghost.

Put the spelling rhyme for *night* beside your picture.

Use the good night message to highlight the *ight* words featured in it.

Make a list of any other *ight* words you know or can find.

busy

It is easy to misspell **busy**, writing it as **bizzy** because of the sounds you hear in it. To help you to remember the **bus** part of **busy**, think of a bus that is busy.

Learn that **bus** + **y** = **busy**

Other **bus** words that can be hard to spell successfully:

business
bus + i + ness = business
(Note the **i** in **business** is silent)

busily
bus + i + ly = busily

bus + y = busy

Draw a bus with lots of people on it to show it is busy.

Write and draw everything that helps you to remember how to spell **busy** successfully, include the word sums for **busy**, **busily** and **business**.

mice

The word **mice** is an example of a word that has **ice** in it. Sometimes you may have put **s** for the **c** in the **ice** part of the word because this is what it sounds like it should be.

If you learn the spelling rhyme below for **mice**, it will help you to remember that it is **c** that goes before **e**, not **s**.

The spelling rhyme for **mice** is:

mice in cracked egg

ACTIVITY

★ Draw two mice in a cracked egg. Then write the spelling rhyme for **mice**.

★ Now write words that rhyme with **mice**, making sure that you write the **ice** part of these words accurately.

★ Write down words with **ice** in them that do not rhyme with **mice**.

mice
i n
c racked
e gg

laugh & cough

The two spelling rhymes below will help you to remember the tricky **ugh** letter pattern in **laugh** and **cough**. In both these words, the **u** is silent and the **gh** gives the **f** sound.

For the spelling rhymes you need to imagine two gorillas. One is an uppity gorilla wearing a posh hat. The other gorilla is naughty and cannot help but

laugh at uppity gorilla's hat.

He laughs and laughs, until he begins to

cough over uppity gorilla's hat.

ACTIVITY

Draw the uppity gorilla wearing a posh hat. Draw the naughty gorilla, who cannot help but laugh at this funny sight. Think of suitable speech bubbles for each gorilla.

Write the spelling rhyme for *laugh*.

Now draw a picture to illustrate when the naughty gorilla begins to cough over the uppity gorilla's hat.

Write the spelling rhyme for *cough* beside your picture.

l augh
a t
u ppity
g orilla's
h at

c ough
o ver
u ppity
g orilla's
h at

27

word & world

When spelling **world**, the **or** part of it is often misspelled.

A good way of being able to spell **world** successfully is to remember that it is **word** with **l** slotted in.

word becomes **world**

Of course, it is all well and good to know that **world** is **word** with **l** slotted in before the final **d**, but for you to be able to use this knowledge effectively, you must have at your fingertips the accurate spelling of **word**.

w ords
o f
r oald
d ahl

If you are in any doubt as to the exact letter pattern of **word**, then use this memory jogger to help you.

As an author, Roald Dahl made his living by his use of words to tell a story. So if you think of the stories that were made from the "**words of roald dahl**", you have this as a reminder for the exact order of letters to spell **word**.

ACTIVITY

Draw a picture of the world. Next write **world** below in bubble writing and colour in the **word** part of it in one colour and the **l** in a different colour.

This will emphasise that **world** is **word** with **l** dropped in before the final **d**.

yachts

A word with a most unusual letter pattern is **yachts**. Because of its strange letter pattern, it is hard to think of the right order of letters in **yachts**.

If you learn the spelling rhyme below, you should have no problem in spelling **yachts**.

The rhyme is: **Yachts are**

yellow and clean hurrying to sea

By using the first letter of each word in the rhyme after 'yachts are', you will be able to spell **yachts** quickly and exactly.

Yachts are

y ellow

a nd

c lean

h urrying

t o

s ea

ACTIVITY

Draw some yachts coming out of a harbour and hurrying to sea. Putting a speed mark behind each yacht would suggest hurrying. The yachts need to be yellow. Think about what you can draw on each yacht to suggest they are clean.

Point to the appropriate part of your picture as you say the spelling rhyme for *yachts*. Learn this rhyme off by heart.

Write and draw everything that helps you to remember how to spell *yachts* successfully.

sword

It is difficult to spell **sword** accurately because the **w** is silent and is left out.

To remember the **w** in **sword**, think of this word sum:

s + word = sword

ACTIVITY

★ Write the word **sword** on two slips of paper. Cut one of the **sword** words into **s** and **word**.

★ Now make the word sum above putting **+** and **=** where needed.

-ight & -ice

Here are some words that have the **ight** or **ice** letter pattern.

Hello. It's me, Bertie, again.

Well, did you enjoy my spelling activities and seeing what I was up to on each page? I hope you have practised and practised how to remember the spelling of all the words in the book. As the saying goes, "Practice makes perfect."

I challenge you now to take Bertie the Magician's spelling challenge. See if you can remember the exact spelling for each of the words. I am sure you will have success. The next step is to use the tricks and tips you have learned to be able to spell more words correctly.

Your spelling vocabulary will have improved immensely whilst you have had fun going through my book. **Now that's magic!**

Look out for further Spelling Magic publications coming soon!

Doodle pad

Draw here,
 write here........
  whatever you like.

Doodle pad

Bertie's
doodle →